Blind Spot

Blind Spot

Susan Eisenberg

The Backwaters Press

Author photo by Simon Eisenberg, copyright Simon Eisenberg, © 2006
Cover photograph copyright Susan Eisenberg © 2006
Cover design by Bristol Creative, www.bristolcreative.com
Book design by The Backwaters Press

Published by: The Backwaters Press
                Greg Kosmicki, Editor/Publisher
                3502 N. 52nd St.
                Omaha, NE 68104-3506
                www.thebackwaterspress.homestead.com
                gkosmicki@cox.net

ISBN: 0-9785782-1-X

Library of Congress Control Number: 2006930063

Acknowledgments

Thanks to editors of the following journals and anthologies where some of these poems, or earlier versions of them, first appeared.

5 AM: "Coma" and "Reduction"
Alaska Quarterly Review: "Heads"
Bridges: "Imagine: My Grandmother Asks About Lori
        Berenson"
Frontiers: "Heirlooms"
Labor: "Remembering the Fire at Triangle Shirtwaist"
Many Mountains Moving: "Funnel Clouds" (previously
        "Aliens")
Mothering: "Introduction to Asthma"
Orion: "Message"
Prairie Schooner: "My Grandmother Hated Jack Ruby,"
        "My Grandmother Hated My Boyfriend,"
        "My Grandmother Hated the Neighbors," and
        "Pocket Billiards"
The Progressive: "Seder Plate"
Pudding: "The Elder"
Sojourner: "Bells of Lowell, 1836," "Details," "Kathy
        Leonard," and "Miscarriage"
Women's Review of Books: "At the Passing of Calamity Jane"
        and "'Parties Must Be Appropriately Dressed'"

Whatever It Takes: Women on Women's Sport (Farrar, Straus),
        "Losing Baseball"

For their nurturance of many of these poems, grateful appreciation to Eleanor Wilner, Larry Levis, Alan Williamson, Tom Lux and the Program for Writers at Warren Wilson College; and to the serenity provided by a residency at Hedgebrook. Thanks to Denise Bergman for her designer's eye. Thanks to Zoe and Simon for their loving honesty, patience and humor

such good luck

out of the air

crossing guard

for Nan, Sally and Kaylyn

such good luck

Heirlooms

She unstitched all remnants
of the girl from the shtetl
and spun our gold into skeins of straw
washed, dyed, and sewn by hand into
her proudest dress, woven
in perfect English: *I was born
in New York City.*

Details

Trained to set plates
properly escorted
on a table that was dressed:
fork   knife spoon
cup with saucer upper right
salad plate left
napkin folded under fork,

I observed, each Tuesday,
my grandma serve lunch to Lillian
who washed woodwork and windows,
ironed and mopped—
without placemat   saucer
or ever
            in her napkin
                        a fold.

My Grandmother Hated the Neighbors

Every Saturday morning, in 3-inch heels
and make-up, her dress hemmed
to the knees, she walked up the driveway
and—right in front of them—started up
her car, then drove to the beauty shop
where, beneath the hairdryer,
that chanting wouldn't be heard.

Was it just to humiliate her
that they prayed outside
wearing long coats and velvet hats,
their sideburns curled like girls,
davening their mumbo jumbo
like it was the Middle Ages
and we lived in a filthy shtetl?

Or, just to shame us all
in front of the *goyim*
that they grew their beards
untamed—like they wanted
someone to yank at them? Pull them
down to their knees and her
—an American—with them.

My Grandmother Hated Jack Ruby

Every word Dan Rather spoke she heard.
The doctor's speech to the press —
by heart. Every replay watched
for the smallest thing new.
Nothing — not a word not a frame —
nothing, she missed nothing. Camped

days in front of the TV
wrapped in her afghan,
meals eaten from a tray,
barely a nap in the chair,
more tears cried than Jackie —
no minutia too minute my grandmother
missed nothing   until

one lousy *fershtingetta* minute
he couldn't wait — before *bang*
he gave Oswald the pop he deserved —
for an old lady to get back from the toity
that stinking son-of-a-gun Ruby.
What? She should soil herself too?

My Grandmother Hated My Boyfriend

All his *pleases   thank you*s
polite answers about school
clearing the dinner dishes—
only evidence against him

as if she needed more proof
than his red curls   green eyes
unzipped voice   to spell out SEX
(though the parents-with-the-fancy-
college-degrees seemed fooled).

When he brought her the last dirty cup
and spoon, she shook soapwater in his face
and said *No wonder your grandmother
died. She must have hated you.*

My Grandmother Hated the Cherry Tree

that should have been ashamed
of itself and died
after lightning struck it twice, but
still blossomed and bore fruit.
Once, as grand and handsome as the husband
America promised, its boughs were short
almost bald, like the man her father arranged.

She paid the next door retarded boy
one dollar to chop it down with his axe.

When the family returned home—such foolish
commotion and carrying on you never heard.
Over an ugly thing.
Too ugly to live in the yard.

My Grandmother Hated College Students

because the boys' beards
were never washed and the girls—
if they wore skirts at all—hemmed them
up to their vaginas and because
for that money   *aiyyyyyyyyyyy*
        you should learn more
        than how to have sex
        without having babies.
And because

she earned her high school diploma first
but the next sister—
the one who smoked cigarettes,
wore pants, shaved her eyebrows,
and changed her birthdate with each new beau—
was the one sent to normal school
even though on her it was a waste.

Monday Afternoons, When It Was My Grandmother's Turn

She'd serve chicken salad, strudel,
and gelatin molded into colored stripes inlaid
with mosaics of canned fruit. Then,
around card tables in our living room:

a tumult of widow's rings and rhinestone jewelry;
powdered noses, red lips, and beauty shop hair;
claims of straight-A grandchildren, and sons-in-law
making bundles in The Market;
the rapid *clack clack clack clack*
of mahjong blocks, or, every five
or ten minutes, a critical chorus
because a wrong canasta card was played.

Even before I closed the back door,
I could feel their pinches
as I was petted and passed around the tables:
better than a photo, more like a charm
on a bracelet you can really touch.

Such good luck: a girl who never

heard: *pogrom.*

Capitalism Takes

Bar Harbor, Maine

I weep for all that's been traded
      watching you dance with your grandmother
      on grass near the ocean, the old dance:
      slow steps
      to drums and chants that echo against a canopy
      of open sky.

Taught public school scorn for natives who sold
Manhattan for $28—a sleight of hand—
we never caught on that
our elders
traded our circle for a place in line; gave away
our best stories
for a card with their name spelled wrong
and a grab bag
          of pennycandy.

      My grandmother never showed me
      that dance she danced on a tabletop
      while her father clapped   a clapping
      that echoed through shtetl rooftops
      against a canopy of open sky.
For those who have passed   and all traded   weep.

Imagine: My Grandmother Asks About Lori Berenson

My grandmother wants to know,
could she send Lori Berenson cookies.
I know she means her chocolate chips
with extra flour so they'll look pretty
(even though they taste dry). I explain, No,
she's in a mountaintop prison in Peru
where they don't allow even a toilet,
no radio or TV, newspapers or magazines,
or glass on the window, or any water except cold—
so no use sending cookies.
But she's already gotten out the baking sheets,
the sifter, and set the oven to 350.
She's tying on her apron and opening the stepstool
to reach the sugar. -Do you think she'd like
extra chocolate chips? she asks. -Remember,
I used to mail you cookies in a Higbee's box
and you'd write how all your friends thanked me?
-Gram, (I had to interrupt) Lori Berenson is not
in a college dorm. She's in Yanamayo Prison
12,700 feet up in the Andes. In solitary.
Her hands and liver are swollen. She's worrying
about frostbite, not pastry in a Higbee's box—

My grandmother, measuring vanilla, gives me a look;
the nest of metal teaspoons, like castanets, shake
in her hand. -Better than you I know the kind of place
where she is. Better than you, Miss American-
Who-Knows-Things-from-Books. She's where
you would have been if I hadn't prayed and cried.
Remember back? I warned you what Aunt Mil said?

That if you didn't watch out, you'd be in
big trouble. And then I asked,
Are you already in trouble? *and you never gave*

an answer. Reach me the walnuts.
I bet she likes walnuts. (And then)
I wish I could send them still warm.

Imagine: My Grandmother Counsels on My Daughter's Boyfriend

In the middle of the road, that yellow jeep
idles
like some wild buck.
Then he rings her
from a phone in   his   pants
and down
              the porch steps
                            she trots.

Even the dopiest pirate—
dangling a gold loop from his eyebrow
to blind himself!—could show manners. My cat
knew
to come to the door,
put out a paw, say, *How do.*

Imagine: My Grandmother Has Her Picture Taken with Netanyahu

While the cameraman fusses, my grandmother
asks Netanyahu: *Why would a man with such
a handsome face act
like a mshuga?* and explains how
in the '20s, she and Nate built
way way out—past the trolley car line,
only transportation automobile—and
the only Jews.
Always I gave the neighbors roses from my garden.

One heart attack. Pffft. I'm a widow with two girls.
Now suppose, Mr. So Smart, I'd been a provoker like you.
Mmmmhhh?

Seder Plate

This year even the charoses tastes bitter,
salt water over everything. Enough

rejoicing at plagues—as though God
uproots olive groves and smites
first-born sons. Let the shank bone signify
orphaned arms and legs.
Let the roasted egg signify
eyes blinded by rubber bullets.
Let the matzo signify peace
without justice: fragile and tasteless.

Keep the door open all night for Elijah.
He has been wandering
since seven tanks swallowed his house in Gaza.

out of the air

The Watch

Her mother gave her a watch. It was a kindness,
but within 2 weeks
the hands vanished. Just like that.

The numerals 1 through 12 still circled.
Otherwise, the square face was bare.

On the chance the lost limbs
were crouched beneath the bezel,
she tried shaking the blankness.

She tried looking away and looking back.

She tried forgiving her mother for all unmotherly deeds.

Remembering how gentleness
could vanish and reappear in her mother's hands,
she kept the watch on her dresser
and checked it each morning when she woke.

Bells of Lowell, 1836

sleep cut open each morning by
clangs of the mill bell, her teeth
ache with each reverberation

all day   bells   bells to work
in the darkness   bells to breakfast
bonnets kept on because quickly again

bells   back to the machines with their loud
tuka-tuka tuka-tuka tuka-tuka
dust thick as the threads they spin

dinner bell, her mouth filling like a dog's
with saliva she rushes with the others
to her place at table, cannot understand

Luanda's words, asks her to repeat but
another bell—everyone stands
still chewing bites of fried pie

again the machines, this the longest stretch
standing, her legs like numb stalks
rooting her to the oily floor

twice more, bells   for supper and bedtime
unless in her sleep she wakes in a sweat—
even in her dreams some nights   bells

Sunday tourists who gawk
at the factory girls   how she wishes they
could feel the clapper in their bones

oh, to awaken to the sun's
breath, the murmur of animals
or her mother's voice at hearth

Rebecca's Ellen Craft

No more my sister than a horse or dog.
She was a wedding gift from Daddy, and left
his home same day as I, following me
like a shadow. She was Mother's
aching tooth, always under tongue, the daily
tea she poured her husband afternoons.

I thought to leave the bitterness behind
when I betrothed. I did not ask
that she be mine. Daddy chose to answer Mother's
plea by signing the budding
of his betrayal to me. I saw a veil
cross Mother's eyes. What do your papers
say of that—so quick to judge us all?

I could have worked her like a mule,
but trained her as a seamstress
(I hear she plied that trade in Boston)
and slept her at the foot of my bed.
She had her own small house. I allowed her
the carpenter William. I understand
his wages bought their steamboat seats
and paid for carriages, hotels, and trains.

Had it been my silver candlesticks
vanished at Christmas,
would I have been
less wrong to want them back?
You glorify Ellen's flight,
her charade: to pass herself
as gentry and William as her slave.
My Friend, what Yankee millgirl could so claim?

Though I was glad to rid myself of her,
whose face and gestures mocked my own,
as though my laugh were hers! — imagine
my sweet surprise when the President
offered his army to bring her
back to the foot of my bed. I put my arm
on his elbow and called him *Gentleman*.
Had he been Satan I would have done the same.

Moses

Hey, isn't that the Promised Land?
one sandslogger shouts, eyes pinned
on the horizon. *We could be there
in a week!*
        But God's Pet sees
only infidels and wiseguys who need
more sand under their feet,
more sun in their eyes.
No   Promised   Land   yet.
40 years pretending manna
tastes like honey wafers.

Oh, every group has a Big Parader
who wants to lead, even though
wandering the desert 40 years
is his best plan; who expects
everyone—and their cattle—
to follow behind his rod. And
be grateful (or, he'll break things).

We'll die in the desert! someone wails.
Basket Baby laughs. That's the plan.
And no dancing
or other fun when he's around either.
40 serious years. After that

any spot   any land without Moses
would seem like holy ground.

The Elder

for Tom McGrath

Scraps of burlap and silk, handfuls
of seawater, stories without
direction, clouds that formed
no definite shape. All these
he rolled between large palms
that farmed Dakota
until gradually we, too,
heard the poems in our fingertips.

Heads

for Renée (Mickey) Scott
of the International Resistance

Always politicals argue.
Even Berlin '42, in a room
seven stories belowground
(as close to hell as Gestapo
could build): the bodies
hanging from the walls—
some by wrists, some by the neck—
won't agree.

The prisoner in the chair is shown photos.

One soon-among-the-dead
signals her (a shake of his head)
into silence. Another
nods for her to tell. Tell anything.

Interview

When mid-detail the teller pivots
into fog or silence and their eyes
finish the tale—

       as in, They gave us bread and grease.
       The grease, I never ate.
       I rubbed it on my head
       hoping
       my hair would grow back. The grease,
       we didn't know, maybe it was from
       a person   their fat

       as in, She was so
       beautiful. They put her on a bed
       of nails. Every question she wouldn't answer,
       Punch

       as in, After the trucks were bombed
       we scattered. They found us in a field,
       we were eating. They said,
       Do you know what has
       happened, how many killed?
       We kept eating

—it is the interviewer's duty to question
if the story stopped for want of telling

or, because the teller
heard   ears   close.

The State: From the Sixties File

The earth is flat. I have seen people pushed
too far fall off its edge. Press your ear against
my skull: their trailing voices still echo.

I have photographs. You might recognize
someone you've wondered about.

I remember J— in my dormroom, the last time
we spoke. His tense posture in the chair.
Expecting my praise would raise its fist with his
for the comrade who understood:
her rape was not a crime

but a thrust for liberation. Something to cheer:
a black man raping a white woman who
walked down the street two blocks from home.
I remember his eyebrows, the fiery tip
of his cigarette, my own mute throat.

Blindfolded, gunbarrel to the temple, *boom*
slump forward *boom* slump forward   *boom*
that one VC shot a thousand times on news
brought to us by Saran Wrap and GE

souring forever off-key on my tongue
the patriotic medley sung from the flag-
flying porch of childhood.

Would they zip
our whole generation
into green bags?

2 AM. Glass breaking above us.
The sheriff and his sharp-toothed dogs
on their way. J— moves we
end the ROTC takeover, blend into the night's
crowd. As we run, floodlights pour white.

(*Dogs!* I almost scream, but—
        jungles seared of green,
        girls seared of skin, Haydee
        Santamaria's brother's eyes on a tray.
My fears: bourgeois as love. Still, *Dogs!*)

Always: on the phoneline:
the *click:* of extra ears.
Every rally, every march:
Gene greets us by name. We joke:
he must be triplets, a camera for brains,

and laugh at mistakes in their files
(always one relationship behind)
like we'd outwitted them
by changing bed partners.

CIA and DD dollars. Even Professor H— on the take.
The exact dimensions of a tiger cage determined by
which department: Mathematics? Psychology? Business?

In bed D— and I feed each other pomegranate seeds and
all night,
wrestle over the justice of killing   for justice.
Leaflets, cow's blood, draft cards: thrust, thrown, burned.

Two men in sunglasses
can't find M—'s door; they call D—
posing as friends, for directions; arrest M—
at his hospital job. For smuggling
from the Island-Not-Supposed-To-Be-On-the-Map:
T-shirts and poetry books.

Left in a jail that would frighten God,
his long red curls shaved to bald,
even the psychiatrist who prescribes LSD
can't bring M— back.

D—'s security check on J— turns up: zip.
J—'s security check on D—: ditto.

Has the French government fallen?
Y— asks. *Not yet* J— reports, *but
soon the Tupamaros should seize Montevideo.*

A billyclub's quick cuff
to the solar plexus   my lungs
airless   for what seems

forever. *Don't worry* Y— calls out
as they yank my hair for the paddywagon photo.
By the time your trial comes up
you'll be underground!

The bail bondsman shows the rifle holster
under his suitcoat and smiles,
Everyone has loved ones.

Can a Yippie trust someone who wears Lenin's
glasses?
        Or a vanguard cadre take serious
a revolutionary who uses his one call from jail
to order from Pizza Bob's?

O—. The small frame of her body appears
ghostlike in the doorway, holding a cane.
The brown flesh of her knee wrapped
with white bandage. Bullet wound.

Asleep in that Chicago apartment
that night when gunfire
blazed through the door
direct for two sleeping men
            wanted dead   at 21
            dead   at 19 (my age then).

When I see O— next it's just her photo,
black-and-white. The headline: *Charged
with Genocide! Out of the Party!*

Her abortion
hawked on the streetcorner
as everybody's business.

*If you plead to A and B we'll drop
Resisting*, the prosecutor says, confusing cases.
Don't have a Resisting, I zing right back
straight out of *American Civics*
Chapter 7: The American Judicial System.

He shrugs. *We can give you one.
You let me know.* And he opens the door.

In a book, a photograph: R—'s mother
cooked in a chair. She wrote him goodbye
and sat for death. Her face is his.

Language pared
to what fits on a button
or sounds good with *Smash!*
The waitress at Pizza Bob's
says how she hates
those buttons   staring like angry faces
across the counter   leaving such
cheap tips.

Every day in court the same judge
sentences the same young man to jail.
Some days the young man's white—
most days he's black. Finally
my turn comes. The lawyer who said
I'd be lucky to get six months
didn't count on Kent State.

Rambling metaphors about lead pipes and marbles,
the judge places in my hands a National Guard rifle,
then shows the whole courtroom
my fingerprint on the trigger.
I walk: probation and a fine.

Why at Kent no warning shots?

The four dead   nine wounded
are warning shots.

Any white kid missing
that message is deaf.

My two hands could have strangled him
he was that close in open motorcar, his starched
throat taunting. Kissinger. Haig. All of them waved.
Open palms swinging   *tock   tock*
like weights on metronome shafts

The earth should have opened and swallowed
their motorcade whole! On that corner
I was animal: rabid wild dog
barely hearing the voice that whispered
Secret Service   Secret Service
It is never   as simple   as it seems.

Kathy Leonard

1)

I knew her well enough to get a phone call—and yes
that front page photo was Kathy. An ironworker
married to an ironworker. Her father
filed the missing person. A neighborwife
twelve days later called police
    (imagine how she must have begged
    her husband to make that call)
and opened the hallcloset to show
a power saw with bits of bone   cartilage   blood

splattered on the safety guard; the Milwaukee saw
her husband had lent to Kathy's who (the day after
Kathy was last seen) loaded heavy bags
into a trash truck then   returned the sawframe

and a brand new 12-inch blade.

2)

If the saw-lender refused to rat, and his friends
forgot they'd dumped a bloodied
mattress   let me tell you
it's that kind of business. We see and turn away.
We're used to covering up, I'm the same. I never told

about the dental clinic wall that should have been
lead-sheathed but—the price of scrap, high—
after inspection the lead was sold. Or,

the community-financed housing where
the Clerk declared a hallway too narrow
by half-an-inch;
ordered carpenters to move the sheetrocked wall;
and was pleased when he remeasured. Fool.
They'd removed the firewall layer of sheetrock and—
to bury that deception—needed me to change
a faceplate. I shrugged, *You know where they are,*
and walked away. Shrugged and walked away

many times. Or, maybe I'd confess to anything

rather than let that murder vibrate its blade
across my bone: few crimes are solo acts.

Losing Baseball

for Connie Wong

Except for fat Peter picked
with the girls and Connie
chosen before even
the best boy, teams were already
boys-first-then-girls when

puberty demanded absolution:
gym teacher as priest denouncing
all we had worshiped—
    arms that cracked balls over
    the left fielder's head, legs
    that sailed around bases,
    and home, before the ball
    reached infield . . . *Not*

feminine! The gym teacher's taunt landed
two stories up, where fifth-grade girls
grouped at the window
batted the epithet among us:
a live grenade
no one dared hold. Below, Connie
scooped a softball out of the air,
whirled it toward second. Double play.

Remembering the Fire
at Triangle Shirtwaist

Roberto in Milwaukee sizes me up, then sidles over
sideways, like a crab, asks if I've
heard about the woman ironworker from Kenosha.
It's no riddle. I read his eyes, pray he'll go mute.
There are two versions to the story,
he says, placing the bait. I bite, he tells.
*She was an apprentice, had two kids, fell from the steel
and died. They say it shows women can't
handle the business, but
guys fall, too.* He waits.

> I ask for the other version, the one I see
> itching at the soft flesh beneath his shell:
> *She asked for a safety harness,
> foreman said she didn't need one.*

And Seattle, the buzz about the new linewomen? Eager
to impress means easy
to fatigue. Send her up and down, up and down, up
down up the pole. Soon her arms
will just
  let
   go. Or,

unbuckle her belt, let her test her wings.

When Labor, at century's start,
bronzed those bales of flaming shirtwaist girls
cascading
out the ninth-floor windows of Asch—

was that not a covenant
that the sky would stop

       dropping

       women?

Marriage: One Tradition

Onto the collarbone, the weight
of iron.

Near the ear, the padlock's
click.

Into the mouth, a metal plate
inserted to quell rebellion;
as it pokes soft palate,
the reflex to gag
halted
by iron spikes against tongue.

Called *scold's bridle*,
hag's harness,
or *brank*, for 250 years
the iron headcage
humbled women
guilty
of gossip,
        slander,
            shrillness,
                cursing, or
invoking God's revenge.

Practical.
A side loop allowed for public
parading, or chaining
to hearth. Some versions
decorative. Elaborate iron
ass ears, pig's snout, or
feathers and beak.

And yet the mind resists.

Obedience

for Noah, eldest of Andrea Yates' five children

At seven, Mama's shepherd boy
knows better than pills or grown-ups
how to chase off wolves
and keep her home.

Mama's little man keeps the small ones
penned and hushed, to be delivered—
lambling first—into Mama's arked hands
and the floodwaters of the tub;

he guards the stilled forms
lined by size upon the bed, a spot
saved for himself at the head.
A good little boy: not one sheep lost.

Vigilance

Logan Airport, Boston

A Mideast profile
and no luggage to check—

the young man behind me
stands out like an unattended suitcase
on this movie set of uniforms, semi-automatics,
and alerts coded by skincolor.

I ask about (just chatty,
stand-in-line talk)
his destination and (oh!)
he's on my fully fueled
over-the-ocean flight.

So I mention
(as though it's no matter)
this matter of   no bags.

His tale is charmingly told—
        frazzled-student-heading-home,
        luggage sent ahead to parents in Saudi—
but suspect, post-9/11.   I nod.
I note the patrol of guards.

In Zurich, we deplane, smile. Credits roll.
Of course there's a sequel, a return flight.

A colleague from Mumbai
will ask that I transport
and mail to her niece in Houston

a wrapped Christmas gift.

(*Yes, no, no, yes*)
I will find an excuse to decline.

The earth, a spinning centrifuge,
our backs against cold steel,

our vision blurred.

AWE

Oh, why in their march
page by page through the dictionary
did they capture this word
to parade on TV,
its shocked letters full screen?

En pointe   at center:
the gentlest of consonants
stands open-armed, upstretched.
Beside it, to the left, right:
our most prominent vowels. Three letters
paused in a halo of silence—
deliberately
vulnerable.

Now, how shall we witness a redwood,
first snow,
or the crown of a newborn's head
reaching light?

Flu Vaccine

Because I have been persistent
and aggressive;
because I have been chumsy, chatty and charming;
because I have mentioned the names of Doctors Bigshot
and Poohbahboobah;
because I have pleaded, let my voice
waver   at Desperation Cliff;
because English is my native tongue

I know
to phone this Friday morning;
to bypass the message that recommends I call
1-800-Spin-You-in-Circles;
to press 3, the live human voice
and inform said voice:
I know 2000 vials of vaccine have arrived.

I present credentials –
chronic this-and-that, upcoming danger,
possible hush-don't-speak-its-name.
The human voice checks. Corroborates.
Finds that Yes,
my name is on the playing grid to compete
against two-year-olds, mothers with AIDS,
my friend with emphysema to win
Most Desperate 2000.
The chosen will be called,
appointments made.
The others, she's not sure, maybe
a letter will come by mail.

This same morning in Fallujah
2-year-olds,
mothers with AIDS,
someone's friend with emphysema,
a woman like me—chronic this-and-that,
upcoming danger, possible
hush-don't-speak-its-name—
hide from election prizes
tossed from the sky.

All this interrupts my lessons.
I am studying kindness of heart,
mindfulness.
I have taken a sacred vow
to ban the word "evil" from my mouth.

But words, too, persevere, pry open the jaw.
There it is, caught between my teeth
where my tongue can't dislodge it.

crossing guard

Message

Along their bare
sun-hidden backsides
the upper torsos of sycamores
flaunt, through the south-facing
skylight, traces of spring's
unwelcome snow. Printed in white
at each bough-fork: my morning's
greeting: Y-Y-Y-Y-Y.

Next of Kin Advice

A police detective calls. From out-of-state.
You hear, *listed as Next of Kin*

and a hospital name. You're sure
he's mistaken but call the number
penciled on the envelope.
The Emergency Room nurse
manages you firmly, *Don't delay.*
You start counting minutes,
beg your way onto the last
available seat
on the only flight left.

Airport to hospital,
then to your mother, 85, almost-blind,
you carry a set of words.
Individually, each could be harmless, but
loaded in order, they're set
to explode: feet grab air.

Before your mother's fully awake,
while she's still on a mattress so there's nowhere
to fall, you tell her

her daughter's been shot in the face
with a sawed-off shotgun
by four men who snatched her purse
in broad daylight.

As soon as you say *shot*
get quick to the end. Add
whatever good news you can.

Coma

On TV, it's a private
bedside scene:
a loved one whispers intimacies and,
with a flicker of eyelids,
the patient awakens into re-cognition
and a duet
of soft-spoken confessions. But here

after midnight, in the only
trauma unit
on Cleveland's East Side,
where I'm brought to a bedside congestion
of tubes and flashing numbers and open wounds,
the nurse instructs, *Speak LOUDLY*
so your sister can hear,
and stays by my side.

I have flown six hundred miles
to be mute. I have no intimacies
to shout. I recite facts

starting with   our names.

Search

Her conscious mind
that failed to arrive by ambulance
with her bloodied body

is needed for questioning
by doctors and detectives.
I'm sent out into the fog,
my voice-that-could-be-hers as lure.
No one is interested in our thorny past
or the years we hardly spoke
or the knife on the kitchen wall.

Only that hours are passing.

Tension begins to clot
dangerously. And then,
after 30 hours trolling the universe,
her mind finds its own way home

when it snags on—*Where's my purse?*
—last memory, and rubs
to smooth the jagged edge from where it broke.
Her bag is not in her hand, *Where's
my purse!?!* And, the very object

that catapulted this horror becomes
the hook to lash
                    for mooring.

Reduction

Through the windows
of the blue van
witnessed prowling down East 126th
that afternoon, it didn't matter

that she'd turned down her friend's
offer of a ride
            to walk in the sun;

or what had been shared over coffee;
or her plans.

A small woman   alone   on foot
carrying a purse—

Miscarriage

I am pregnant only with
                    a melancholy
that sits in my womb: a stubborn child
unwilling to be budged by my daughter's laughter,
my husband's caresses, friends' consoling words,
or the folding of one day
                    into the next.

O my sweet neverborn.

The womb, plundered raw, aches
for this not-yet-being
the womb
        alone
              knew by touch.

A grief that begs pardon, coughs
quietly, aware
even in raging moments
                    of its slimness;
a grief that *means* to be small,
but grows fierce and unforgiving:

a mother's mourning.

O my sweet neverborn
for you my life stood ready.

Introduction to Asthma

Cacophony rising in his lungs,
oxygen level falling,
the muscles in his chest outmatched
by fists tightening around his airways

my seven-year-old son believes
he will die

        but

Anyone who wants to kill me he says
would have to kill my Mom
first. If I went to Heaven, she'd
go with me. If I went to Hell,
she'd go with me. A stretcher
wheels him toward an ambulance—
not the time for lessons on Death's

disregard for protocol
and preference. I hug his eyes in mine
and breathe for both our lives.

Public School at Open House

Parents tour the carcass
of classrooms picked clean
by the pennysavers.
The science teacher
needs paper cups.
The kindergartens:
paint. No red
in September,
by October:
no yellow.
Trees   grow bare.
Bulletin boards
sprout pictures
with no sun.

Funnel Clouds

A permission slip
thrust at me after cereal
to be signed
before the race to the bus
ends, *Police escort has been requested.*
The morning's headline: 17-Year-Old
Stabbed to Death (blocks from our house).

Today's signature will not be rushed
by an 8-year-old

who strokes tears from my face meaning,
Just sign it Mom. Time to go.
I mutter about days when school groups
singing Christmas carols
did not need armed protection,
and grandmothers were not shot
walking their boys home from school. She nods,

holding my hand like a friendly crossing guard
at a dangerous intersection, coaxing me
unwilling, into her day
while I, like Aunty Em beside the storm cellar,
holler her name into the winds.

"Parties Must Be Appropriately Dressed"

ends the letter
with my court date
for divorce, suggesting
a fashion line for The Uncoupling Woman.

Simple black with veil
for the Truly-Bereaved
among us, the Still-Sure-
We-Could-Make-It-Work-ers.
Or how about a sackcloth number—
traditional, in beige?

A Thank-God!-er might consider
re-tailoring her wedding dress
as a housecoat seamed with velcro.
Once the final judgment's
decreed: whip it off, wave it around
and tie that thing to the car bumper
for a honking tooting ride through town.

For the Sainted-Mothers-
Married-to-Real-Shmoes
there'd be pastel sweatsuits
that could be embossed
with large color photos
of the children he neglects
staring wistfully at him
from her bosom.

For the Realistic
there'd be power suits. A-line
skirts and matching jackets
in neutral with pearls. This is
business. What's negotiated for yourself
and the children is on paper.
Expect   nothing more.

Consider wearing work clothes.
A full suit of armor. Something
chaste. Something low-cut.
What you wore when you met him—
inside out. Find your look. Try:
Elegant. Sporty. Worn Thin.

And shoes. Step into spiked heels.
Steel-toed boots. Dancing slippers.
Accessories speak. Wear those earrings
from his mother. Or your grandmother-
who-thought-you-deserved-the-best's
cameo brooch. A headdress. A wig.
A clown corsage that squirts water.
Something your daughter made.
Something your son gave you.
Think color. Think texture.
You have been asked for a statement.

Sarah's Grief

The kindling wood. The mountain.
From the beginning it was meant
to be. The boy led by the hand. The boy
bound on the altar. The knife
raised above the boy and then—the ram

hidden offstage until just that moment.
To make a man of the boy:
mirror of blade above his widened eyes.

From that day forward and forever
Isaac will have his own ram ready
to push in his place: *God
made me do it* or   some woman;

and Isaac will know—
        with all "the stars of heaven"
        and all "the sand which is on the seashore"
        his witness—to run
from the reach of familiar hands.

The Mammo Tech

Compressing my left breast between glass,
she tries to keep the chatter
light: weather, change-of-season
colds, her daughter's first birthday, but—
Hold your breath   Okayrelax—

the breast reduction of her niece, just 19,
won't leave the room. *A 44D, but I didn't think*
hers were bad. I mean, I see them all day.
Should have been routine. Two days later,
in the shower, passes out. Blood clot in her brain.

The machine twists cockeyed. With firm hands
she repositions me for the next angle: one arm
up, other shoulder back,
arranging my breast neatly on the plate;
then glides behind the screen
while I wonder how to shield the breasts budding
beneath my daughter's blouse.

Pocket Billiards

After fifty years of vacations
postponed   holidays worked   dinners
kept warm—
        years with two seasons:
        Tax and Not Tax—
my father at 82 retires
to classes   travel   and since
the stroke   aqua aerobics.

I'm volunteering at a nursing home he announces
Thanksgiving. *I teach pocket billiards*
to Mrs. Wojciechowski. Woy-shih-kof-skee.
He speaks her name with a peasant's
memory for thick barley soup   dark
chewy bread   root vegetables smelling
of damp earth. *I knew a Wojciechowski*

when we lived on 79ᵗʰ —where names bulged
with z's and k's and j's, where he was born
fourth of six in a back-of-the-store apartment,
where the streets marching past Eisenberg Hardware
Sowinski   Kosciuszko   Pulaski honored
Polish generals of the American Revolution:
more important there than Lafayette.

But at McGregor's Nursing Home
named for the Irish barrel-maker
who struck wealth holding John D.'s oil,
they call Mrs. Wojciechowski
Irene W   skipping
the syllables my father savors.

My game isn't what it used to be. Precisely
angled shots   nimble click of ball
on ball interrupted by War   five decades
at a desk   arthritis. His own slate pool table
nine by five   with sloping pockets
gone   when he returned after Armistice—
his father's donation to the USO.

He plays pool now on the table
at McGregor's. With Mrs. Wojciechowski
who has carpal tunnel syndrome.
On Tuesdays.

Another Stroke

With a quick twist-tug he once more
outwitted Death, that runt, when it grabbed him
firm by the calf and pulled.

He danced a little jig to disguise the limp, threw in
some soft shoe to make the cane
look like costume, shot pool with the cue stick

behind his back! The grandkids should know:
he can still ricochet the 10-ball into the 7 so it drops
like a baby into the side pocket.

Six Red X's

My own arms, not strong enough to hold
my father's dead weight—
an attendant, a kind stranger in her twenties,
helps him stand,
         undress,
         toilet;
and leads him, dressed in hospital gown,
to a bed she surrounds with gym mats

in case, tonight, he leaves
to pick up tax returns at 105th and St. Clair;
or to head home to his wife.

      My ballast, what voice is there
      to follow, now,
      into the light of six red X's?

I sit beside him,
stroking his head as sleep
relaxes his face from the day's efforts.
Then lay my head against his chest.

I must have expected his heartbeat,
to be halting and off-kilter
like his walk; or, like his speech,
to strain between long silences.
But it's steady, intent,
like his voice beside me that afternoon,
stopped at the bottom of Cedar Hill and Euclid
facing into six red X's
in lights two-foot high across all
six lanes of Carnegie: guardians
of Cleveland's rush hour.
From the back seat my mother

said what was sensible, Take a right.
Take Chester.

But you glanced at your watch and told me
to go straight. Take Carnegie.
She repeated—louder, insistent—Go right!
You repeated, calmly—

and so softly I had to strain to be sure—
Go straight. The lights will change for you.

As I drove through limbo
in the curb lane of a ghostly Carnegie
expecting a head-on,
the six red X's hung firm
past 105th, past 79th.
We were almost to 30th
when two red X's turned green.

The Hammock

Groggy mornings, sleepless 3 AMs,
late afternoons when "no one understands,"
you find your way into the swaddling
of colorful thread cast
like a spider's web between pine tree
and the abandoned swingset.
Around you, the camouflage of blossoms:
hydrangea, astilbe, day lilies, phlox.
Above: green arches of maple, branch
over branch—each leaf
full with summer—like the breezy canopy
of a baby's cradle.

Exhaust Fan

Teenage boys bunched in the bathroom
keep the exhaust fan motor running:
the getaway driver, counted on
to inhale,
then deliver into the anonymity
of afternoon air, the smoke

exhaled
from a circle of lips
where hairs, awkwardly shaved,
sprout like trouble.

Maintenance

The walls that shoulder our home—
    below the kitchen, stone over stone;
    the rest, bricks laid course upon course—
have grown weary. Even small storms leak past
their sentry. North, south, east, west: the basement's wet.

Cracks and gapes must be scraped clean,
re-mortared, each square foot of wall
skinned with a sealant to make once again shiptight
the brick and stone set here a hundred years past.

Old mortar, beneath the press
of steel brush, turns to dust. Rituals
of repair—mostly tedious tasks—
cement generations to one foundation.

Driver's Ed

1) Check Brakes

Aware that the ominous signs—*Falling Rocks
Moose Crossing   Low Flying Aircraft   Bridge
Slippery When Wet   Left Lane Ends*—are decoys,
she grips the steering wheel in a white-knuckle
deathhold   ready to swerve   ram into reverse
or leap from her moving car or career:

her shoulders braced for the unposted
disaster about to veer in
from her blind spot.

2) Dead End

For no reason
anyone can see, she ignores
back-seat shouts
and wild handwaving from the roadside,
certain she's found a shortcut no one knows.
Years later *I mean*

years later she'll notice: the asphalt's ended:
The End: no further can go.
Sit in disbelief with the motor running. And finally

turn around. Head back to start where
sure enough there'll be a sign
standing plumb
plain as plain
letters so clear a dog or cat could read:
Don't bother down this road. Nothing here.

3) Overlook

Every turnout, she pulls over and —
everyone's got to climb out of the car.
Miles still to drive, and she brings out a goddamn
picnic. Plaid blanket. Cups of lemonade.
Sandwiches cut triangular. Grapes.

Or, sometimes just sits on the grass

smiling

until you quit saying
we need to get going
we need to get going
don't we need to get going

and notice how the blue lupines
brush cheeks   whenever wind
offers the slightest excuse

and put your head in her lap to watch clouds.

At the Passing of Calamity Jane

Mebbe she married the Prince of Pistols, mebbe not.
And the ambush story, folks here tell that lots of ways.
The girlbaby — I wouldn't know. Y'see, with hail the size
of coffee cups, winters so cold your eyeballs near froze,
gold making folks jumpy as mountain goats, and craziness
at times a woman's best protection — most trails led
through switchbacks of tale and truth.

But whether she were mule-skinner and scout
or whore and drunk, don't matter none.
She'd a-shared her last grub
or stake with any soul Luck tossed out.
She loved her Satan, but when the oats
was gone, she shoo'd him to the hills.

Here's a fact.
I saw it meself. *She rode
the most dangerous trails   upside down.
Head on the saddle, boots to the sky.*

Notes

My Grandmother Hated Jack Ruby (p. 16)

Witnessed by millions of viewers, the murder on November 24, 1963, of Lee Harvey Oswald, accused assassin of President Kennedy, by nightclub owner Jack Ruby in the basement garage of the Dallas police station, was the first homicide to be broadcast live on network television.

Imagine: My Grandmother Asks About Lori Berenson (p. 22)

US citizen and human rights activist Lori Berenson has been imprisoned in Peru since her arrest in 1995, shortly after her 26th birthday. First sentenced by a secret military tribunal to life imprisonment for treason, she was retried in 2001 and sentenced to 20 years. She denies all charges.

Rebecca's Ellen Craft (p. 32)

In 1848, Ellen and William Craft escaped from slavery in Georgia—where she was owned by her biological half-sister, Rebecca—by openly traveling North disguised as a white male slaveowner (Ellen) and his slave (William). The Crafts' bold journey made them celebrated among abolitionists. When the Fugitive Slave Act became law two years later, they were to be its first victims but escaped from Boston to England, returning to the US during Reconstruction.

Heads (p. 36)

Renee (Mickey) Scott (1906-2005) was awarded the Belgian Medal of Honor for her work in the International Resistance as a courier between Paris and Brussels. Captured by the Gestapo in 1941, she spent four years in the Ravensbruck concentration camp.

The State: From the Sixties File (p. 38)

Haydee Santamaria, a leader of the Cuban revolution, was captured along with her brother Abel in the July 26,1953 attack on the Moncada Barracks. Under interrogation by Batista's soldiers, she was shown a bleeding human eye and told that it was Abel's; she is said to have responded, "If you tore his eye out and he did not speak, neither will I."

In a pre-dawn attack December 4, 1969, that was part of national COINTELPRO operations, 21-year-old Fred Hampton, chairman of the Illinois Chapter of the Black Panther Party, was murdered by Chicago police; Mark Clark was also murdered and six others injured. A floor plan with an X marking Hampton's bed had been provided by an informant to the FBI. Ballistic evidence showed that of the nearly 100 bullets shot, only one could have been fired by the Panthers. A charismatic leader, Hampton had formed a multicultural alliance among various Chicago gangs, which he termed a "rainbow coalition."

Kathy Leonard (p. 44)

The first successful murder conviction in Massachusetts without a body was the case of ironworker Kathy Leonard Romano (1959-1998). Her husband was convicted of second-degree murder for killing her and dismembering her body in front of their 2-year-old son.

Remembering the Fire at Triangle Shirtwaist (p. 47)

On March 25, 1911, 146 garment workers, mostly women and girls, died in a fire at the Triangle Shirtwaist Co. located in the Asch Building on Manhattan's Lower East Side. Because the factory doors were locked, many jumped from the ninth floor to their deaths.

AWE (p. 53)

Intended to leave the enemy in "shock and awe" and "paralyze its will to carry on," Rapid Dominance, a military concept developed by Harlan Ullman and James Wade at the National Defense University of the United States, argues for immediate, overwhelming and "spectacular displays of power," such as at Hiroshima and Nagasaki. Employed by George W. Bush in the 2003 invasion of Iraq, it was expected to eliminate the need for a ground war.

A note on the cover

The cover photograph by Susan Eisenberg is of an afghan handmade by her grandmother, Elizabeth Shatsky Weltman Shifrin.

About the Poet

Raised in a three-generation household in Cleveland, Susan Eisenberg lives in Boston. She is the author of the poetry book, *Pioneering* (1998), and the nonfiction book, *We'll Call You If We Need You: Experiences of Women Working Construction* (1998), which was selected as a *New York Times Book Review* Notable Book and optioned by MGM for a feature film. Licensed as a master electrician, she helped shape the cultural expression and analytical thinking of the tradeswomen's movement nationally and internationally. Currently she is developing *Perpetual Care*, a photo-based exploration of the relationship between the chronically ill and medication. She travels widely as a poet and lecturer; and teaches at the University of Massachusetts Boston.

Printed in the United States
57706LVS00004B/1-228